WORDS & QUILTS

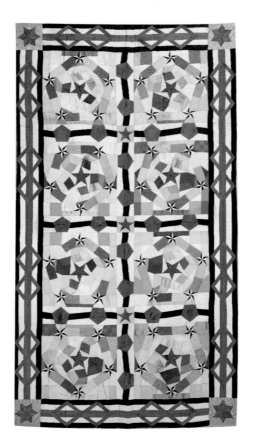

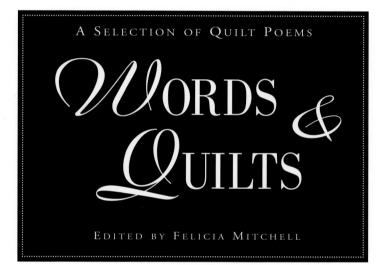

A SELECTION OF QUILT POEMS

Words & Quilts

EDITED BY FELICIA MITCHELL

THE QUILT DIGEST PRESS

Simply the Best from NTC Publishing Group

Lincolnwood, Illinois U.S.A.

Editorial and production direction by Anne Knudsen.

Book and Cover Design by Rick Dinihanian and John Lyle,

    Green Lizard Design, St. Helena, CA.

Photography by Sharon Risedorph, San Francisco.

Book editing by Judy Franklin.

Manufactured in Hong Kong.

Library of Congress Cataloging-in-Publication Data

Words & quilts : a selection of quilt poems / edited by Felicia

Mitchell. — 1st ed.

    p. cm.

ISBN: 0-8442-2644-0 (hardcover) :

1. Quilts—Poetry. 2. Quilting—Poetry. 3. American

poetry—20th century. 4. Quilts—Pictorial works. I.

Mitchell, Felicia, 1956-. II. Title: Words and quilts.

PS595.Q48W67 1994

811'.54080357—dc20   94-38673

                         CIP

Published by The Quilt Digest Press,

a division of NTC Publishing Group,

4255 West Touhy Avenue,

Lincolnwood (Chicago), Illinois 60646-1975, U.S.A.

To My Parents

·····································

John A. and Audrey E. McClary Mitchell

The quilts hanging on my quilt rack are a legacy from my family dating back to 1835. My two favorites are unfinished quilt tops.

One is pieced from the dresses I wore from the fifth grade through college. Looking at it, I see more than strawberries on blue checked fields, madras, or dotted swiss. I see myself wearing fishnet stockings for the first time or seated on a piano bench for a recital or moving into my first apartment. As I work to turn this top into a quilt, I assure my mother that the uneven patches she apologizes for are very special to me.

The other quilt top, which will remain unfinished, is a crazy quilt from the turn of the century. Its embroidery intrigues me, but not so much as the fact that the quilt was never completed. What happened to the quilter? I don't know, but I like to imagine that she, my kinswoman, was a very busy woman. The quilt's mystery feeds my poetic soul.

My love of quilts and of poetry led me to create *Words & Quilts*. It is meant for people who love to gaze at quilts and to see special meanings within them.

Felicia Mitchell

CONTENTS

viii

ACKNOWLEDGMENTS

*M*any people helped me through this project.

I am indebted to the poets who are represented in this book for their connection to quilts. The poets also helped by responding promptly to my correspondence and by proofing their poems. Perhaps for some readers this collection will be an introduction to a poet's work, and poets will acquire new readers.

The curators and registrars of the collections represented enabled me to examine a variety of quilt collections across the United States. The delightfully friendly art world included, but was not limited to, the following, in no special order: James T. Reynolds and Mario Klimiades of the Heard Museum, Phoenix; Cheryl Kennedy, of the Early American Museum in Mahomet, Illinois; Mike Hudson, Kentucky Historical Society, Frankfort; Janey Fire, Museum of American Folk Art, New York City; Polly Laffitte of the State Museum, Columbia, South Carolina; Colleen Callahan, The Valentine Museum, Richmond, Virginia; Rebecca Huffstutler, the Witte Museum; Robert Cargo, Robert Cargo Folk Art Gallery, Tuscaloosa, Alabama; and Doris Bowman, Textiles Division, Smithsonian Institution, Washington, D.C.

Other quilts came from individuals and collectors. I discovered the quilt by Kathy Marx of Nolensville, Tennessee, at the American Quilt Showcase in Pigeon Forge, Tennessee, in 1993, and Kathy Marx arranged for photography. Poets Sandra McPherson and Marilyn Nelson Waniek arranged to have personal quilts photographed. Eli Leon trusted me with many slides from his collections at the onset of my project and arranged for photography.

At different phases, different individuals offered important advice and/or help: Anne Knudsen, The Quilt Digest Press; Thelma Hutchins, Director of Kelly Library, Emory & Henry College; Leslie Justice Cook, quilter and quilting teacher, Haydenville, Massachusetts; Thaylene Pinnock, William King Regional Arts Center, Abingdon, Virginia; Julie Springer, Arlington, Virginia; Charles T. Mitchell, Arlington, Virginia; Rodes Fishburne, Ivy, Virginia; and Amy Littrell, New York City.

Last but not least, my husband Barry Love helped in many ways: listening to my dreams and schemes, proofing, sharing his computer when mine broke down, and commenting on drafts.

WORDS & QUILTS

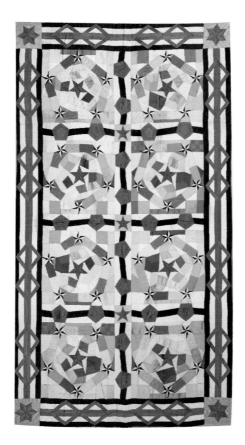

W hen I make a quilt, I lay out the pieces on the floor in different configurations until I decide what works. My son Guy likes to help. Together, we play with this large puzzle for days as I examine the arrangement of blocks to decide if I have created a whole out of all the parts, or if I still have lots of parts with no sense of a whole. When the quilt top feels right, I am ready to sew.

Putting together this book was a good bit like making a quilt. I solicited and received hundreds of poems to review. How did I decide what configuration to use? First, each poem had to fit my vision of the book, and that vision in the beginning was just as inchoate as my own poems are before they reach the page. I knew, however, that I wanted poems with strong images, the feel of the particular, a love of the art of quilting or quilts.

Reading poems helped the inchoate become more real. Selecting the poems involved finding ones that would work together to contribute to the vision, and work individually to evoke the wonder of quilts. The poems I chose are examples of poetry engaged with quilts.

The poets themselves comprise a patchwork, as the short biographies of the contributors at the end of the book suggest. Just as quilters have arisen from every social strata, with their quilts as much telling stories about families and cultures as about color and design, the poets come from many different backgrounds. Included are Americans with colonial and Amish and Appalachian roots, children of immigrants, Native Americans, African Americans. The multicultural range in my book is proof that poets are as varied as calico.

After I selected the poems, I began contacting collectors, galleries, and museums across the country to find quilts to accompany them. I wanted the book to contain, as it does, a cross-section of large museums, small museums, galleries, individual collections. This cross-section is indicative of how quilts come to be seen by the general public. Quilts are family heirlooms, museum treasures, contemporary art, household goods.

Some quilts I visited, others came to me via catalogs, others were selected as helpful people read my list of images and suggested slides for viewing. My slide collection grew like the pile of cotton squares I make as I'm beginning a quilt. Selecting candidates for illustrations was like rummaging around in a cloth store. All the while, my vision of what I wanted grew stronger.

As I collected the many options, I read and reread the poems again and again. I knew I would not simply match up quilt patterns with patterns mentioned in the poems, though that was a starting point. I also wanted to match the spirit of the poem with the spirit of its quilt illustration. Sometimes, viewing a quilt would help me to understand a poem better. Just as often, a poem would help me to read a quilt.

In a few cases, the quilts and poems are exact matches. The quilts inspired the poems. More commonly, I picked up on a quilt image in a poem, or a feeling, or a line. The quilts selected are to enhance, not simply to illustrate.

My hope is that the reader of this book sees the poems and quilts as complementary. A quilt can help with visualization

of a poem, just as a poem can help one to make sense of a quilt. Sometimes the relationship between a quilt and a poem is quite obvious. Other times, the relationship is more subtle. Just as a quilt is constructed of a variety of pieces, this book holds a variety of poems and images, quilts and symbols. The poems and quilts selected represent both tradition and innovation, symmetry and asymmetry, the sentimental and the real.

A Sense of Connectedness

In this book we see tributes to diverse heritages, recognition of familial and cultural ties, homage to particular quilts, attention to the construction and the art, and descriptions of what it is like to lie under a quilt. The many voices represented in the poems—from pioneer women to our contemporaries—converge to represent the people behind the quilts. Quilts help people to keep warm both physically and spiritually, the poets seem to say.

Quilts by Stephen Corey catalogs patterns familiar to pioneer women. This catalog of quilt patterns is balanced by a first-person narrative that shares bits of pioneer life and folklore: "A broken thread, a crop gone bad; a twisted stitch, a baby dead." The interplay between the monologue of the woman and the quilt patterns shows how quilts can mark special points in personal history. If they are to play such a role, too, women must start quilting young, as this narrator did, at "only five."

Rose Wreath that accompanies Corey's poem was chosen to illustrate the pioneer spirit of the poem. Made by the Leyendecker family of Columbus, Texas, circa 1890, this quilt shows a folk element borne of independent thinkers. Notice the minor variations in the leaf and rose patterns that add subtle variety to the apparent symmetry of the nine-patch design. This variety is not due to carelessness. As Corey's narrator says, "A broken thread, a crop gone bad; a twisted stitch, a baby dead."

Another poem in the voice of a woman from an earlier time is Suzanne Underwood Clark's *Morning Chore*. Also in the voice of a first-person narrator whose memory is sparked by the sight of a quilt, the poem presents symbols that move the reader from a recognition of death—symbolized by the bent trees of life on a folded quilt—to the need to persevere and "get on with the spinning." Hope is symbolized by dreams of a quilt that is full of wondrous, multiple patterns. A third quilt in the poem is the quilt that covers the narrator at night, one whose leaf pattern allows the narrator to associate the quilt with fun times playing with her mother in the leaves. The tone of this poem connects despair and wonder.

An unfinished quilt top, circa 1870, entitled Sample of Blocks, Unfinished Quilt Top, by Iora Almina Philo Pool, captures well the dreams of the narrator that reveal "stars and plumes, lilies, thistles, cat tracks: emblems of wonder frozen at my waking." The triangulated pattern of Tree of Life is on one of the sample blocks.

A sense of connectedness among quilters is implicit in many poems about quilts and enhances the theme of heritage.

For example, *Written on the Back of a Laurens County Map* by Elizabeth McDade is about the quilts of the narrator's grandmothers. The quilts in the poem are spread across the grass, where the narrator and her mother have laid them. There, washed and drying, the quilts present not only an array of patterns but also the mysteries of four generations. Details from the lives of ancestors can be read between the thread lines: Mama Juliet, Tanny, Brook, Jack, Mary Belle, and more. The quilts are the people. As McDade writes, "All of my people lying on quilts in the sun, somehow all on this earth, on the grass, in the summer morning."

Irish Chain is from South Carolina, made circa 1845 by Eliza Huger. It combines the traditional chain effect of the quilt pattern with a colonial flavor reinforced by the adaptation of the pattern and the colors. Although Eliza Huger's quilt is hung in a museum and not lying on the grass to dry, it is one link in a chain of people from an old South Carolina family.

Deborah Browning's *Repairing the Heirloom* shows how generations may be literally connected by a quilt. Its narrator remarks about a Spider Web pattern that needs repair: "My stitches met hers and I knotted the thread of this net that would catch another generation of small hands, clenching in sleep and letting go." Within this quilt, the narrator recognizes her grandmother in pieces from aprons and faded dresses and then adds herself in the form of a piece from an "old sundress."

Spider Web by African-American quilter Ida Jacobs, from the fifties, is a remarkable quilt that shows the intricacies of this

6

particular pattern and the frugal nature of the quilter as exemplified in Browning's poem. This pattern is ideal for salvaging and transforming so many small pieces of cloth.

Carole Boston Weatherford has written about how someone transformed "scraps too gay to be dustcloths, rescued from the ragman and reborn." Her *Patchwork* presents a catalog of quilt patterns as it reveals a woman whose long life is embodied in the quilts from her life: "Draping her lap, a quilted geography, terrain of textures; valleys at her fingertips and Glory beyond."

By an unknown quiltmaker from New Hope, Pennsylvania, 1875-1900, Crazy Quilt Within Contained Borders shows how small pieces of cloth can be lovingly transformed into religious symbols. With its Cathedral Windows effect, this quilt was selected to illustrate the "Glory beyond" of Weatherford's poem and the quilter's ability to transform.

The way in which quilts can both literally and symbolically connect generations is also addressed in Andrew Hudgins' *Patchwork*, which embodies the magic of transformation. In this first-person poem, the narrator speaks of "crude quilts" made from scraps with jerky stitches that seem to symbolize the manner of a loving but brusque grandmother. The grandmother and grandchild are connected by the grandchild's pilfering of scraps from work and the grandmother's stitches that "yielded a Drunkard's Path."

While Ellen Nelson Pearson's 1910 Drunkard's Path does not exhibit the "crude" and "bad work" of Hudgins' quilt, it does illustrate the effect of the semicircular design. While the pattern may seem of a rambling nature, it is in fact very precise. Note how pieces lock and how the quilting adds depth. This quilt exercises the eye.

Like the poems by Browning and Corey, Ann Struther's *Mother's Postage Stamp Quilt* combines frugality and transformation. It focuses on the creativity and daring of Anna Smith Mohr, who combined her scraps with some store-bought fabric to create a work of art: "In a house without any pictures, this was her picture, her quilting stitches as tiny as secrets, pattern on pattern which only the knowing eye could see."

Postage Stamp Quilt by an unknown quiltmaker accompanies Struthers' poem and shows the minute precision of a quilter working with the tiny pieces of fabric that originate in frugal homes where every piece of cloth is accounted for by women who save money "from selling eggs to buy a little fabric."

Joan McMillan's *Annabelle Cain McMillan* remarks on the frugal nature of quilters but extends the recognition of a thrifty heritage to a recognition of more affluent times. In the second person, it is a poem of address. As the narrator addresses the grandmother, we learn about the hard times of her past through the details of memories. The poem juxtaposes the hard times of the past and the relative affluence of today by contrasting the frugal quilting of "threadbare clothing and flour sacks" of the grandmother with the more extravagant patterns of the granddaughter. This poem is a memorial and an affirmation of self.

McMillan's poem is a fitting companion to Kathy Marx's contemporary quilt Make New Friends, But Keep the Old.

Reinforcing the contrast between the hard times of our ancestors and the relative affluence many share today, Marx's quilt combines traditional patterns with images of outer space. The rich and sparkling cloth embodies the joy of the last two lines of MacMillan's poem: "I take the small cold steel of a needle in my hand, stitch patterns your life would not let you imagine."

Just as quilts themselves can connect generations, the act of quilting invokes a legacy that is passed on. Like a number of the poems, Anne George's *Quilting* shows how women learn from their grandmothers: "We sit at the frame, three women backstitching eight stitches to an inch the way our grandmother taught us." In this poem, as in many poems about quilts, we see the image of the sun, this time reflected in the "thimbles blinking light across the pattern." The peacefulness of this poem captures the special time women have together when they are freed from family obligations to work on their craft.

Four Patch and Triangles Combination by Barbara Zook Peachey from Mifflin County, Pennsylvania, circa 1910, illustrates the alternating triangles of George's poem. The triangle pattern echoes the three women of the poem, whereas the colors within the tightly constructed blocks evoke the mood of the room.

The Quilters by Dorothy Wall reiterates the theme of peacefulness found in stolen time implicit in George's poem. Wall writes about the patience of quilters, of time stolen while children sleep. "Patience, obedience, stillness," says the narrator. "The skies compose our laps." The hands of the quilters become like magic wands in the first stanza.

The precision of stitching that is remarked on in Wall's poem is clearly evident in Pinwheel, with Stuffed Work by an unknown Maryland quilter, circa 1812. The patience threaded into the stuffed work of this quilt picks up some of the patterns mentioned in the poem. Notice especially the grapes. Details such as this embody the patience and diligence Wall expresses in her poem.

Although many poems about quilts celebrate the handiwork of women within their families, many quilts in earlier times were made by slaves for families other than their own. While slaves made quilts of traditional patterns for their owners, the quilts they made for themselves were by necessity patched together from scraps but were by design symbolic of unique interpretations of African art. *Quilt Sutra: "Underground Railroad" (Early 1800s)* by Susan Kelly-Dewitt commemorates the "headache blues, bone-splitting indigo patches; slats of bruise yellow zigzagged on" of a slave quilt, as distinguished from a slave-made quilt. The words of the poem give the quilt vibrant colors more colorful than the few slave quilts that remain, because their constant use has washed so many out and used most of them up. Thus Kelly-DeWitt's poem stands in place of these quilts as a memorial in words. Few actual slave quilts remain today because they simply wore out.

Kelly-DeWitt's poem also shows how slave quilts acted as prayers that "a slave owner's conscience might be pricked and a shred of gospel respect bleed through." The African-American narrative quilt, The Crowded Cross by Yvonne Wells, uses the medium of the quilt for a message that speaks out of the heritage of remembered slavery, just as quilts were once used as signs of the underground railroad. The haphazard patchwork foreground of the found quilt top echoes the zigzags of Kelly-DeWitt's poems and provides a homemade background to the cotton narrative elements of the doves and crosses.

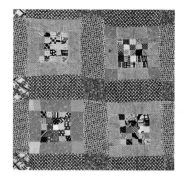

Cross-cultural influences and African-American connections can be seen in the works of contemporary quilters. Sandra McPherson's *Quilt Top Discovered at the Muskogee Flea Market and Found to Contain Blocks Resembling Certain Designs of Descendants of Maroons in Suriname* expands on exactly what the title states. Written in response to an actual quilt top McPherson found, the poem gives the reader some of the mythology of Suriname evoked by the images of the American quilt. This is another poem about how a quilt is metaphorically like a poem, and vice versa.

Quilt Top Found in Muskogee, Oklahoma, circa 1930, presents, as McPherson describes it, "unblending plaid compilations, like gourd heaps or melon stripes rolled into a mound." Notice how the quilt top renders "unlike prints similar" and prints "sewed…back together to clash." Also note the "handwriting of close, irreproachable stitches."

Another shared cultural motif is mentioned in Joseph Bruchac's *Walking in November Across the Stream to the Sweat Lodge*. The narrator mindfully states, "No great issues this morning, no more to do than burn tobacco, speak words by the fire pit, strip the blankets from the sweat lodge." The serenity of the narrator can be read in his reaction to an old quilt whose batting has been stolen by mice "to weave into nests." The narrator accepts that stage in the quilt's life and notes the beauty of the light that "shines through its patterns of red and orange, a sudden flower."

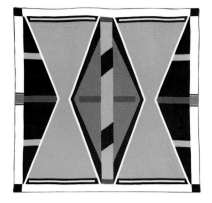

While tobacco is generally condemned in today's society, it has a mythic place in the rituals of the past as a drug that centers the mind. Reminding us of both the indigenous people of the United States and colonial American commerce, the nineteenth-century Tobacco Leaf Pattern quilt presents a tobacco leaf stylized by settlers as a quilt motif. Pairing a southern quilt of Tobacco Leaf Pattern with a poem about a Native American ritual shows how images connect and transcend cultures.

My own poem *How to Read a Quilt* grew out of a reaction to a less widely known motif from Native-American culture embodied in Margaret Wood's Quilt, Crow Martingale Design. Fascinated by the way this quilt had picked up the motif of a harness, and confused initially by how I was to interpret the quilt because I felt illiterate about the imagery of the culture out of which the image came, I wrote the poem to reconcile the confusion and the appreciation.

To understand the quilt, with its geometric hourglass design, I had to find a new way of seeing that was not based on my own cultural lens. Art quilts, like art in general, require the viewer to stand back and take in the whole to begin understanding the parts. Wood's quilt is made of stark contrasts of triangular and narrow rectangular shapes, with bright colors offset by a black that adds dimension. The quilt embodies the ceremonious nature of the martingale. "Stand back and note geometry of line," the poem suggests.

As my experience suggests, often quilts—like paintings or sculpture—invite myriad interpretations and inspire awe and wonder. *The Quilt Show* by Gray Jacobik, set at a quilt show, recognizes the industrious nature of quilters and the variety of patterns. The profusion of images from the quilts in the room is celebrated. To buffer the sense of artistic distance a show might engender, the narrator observes as she stands in a room of quilts that a quilt might say, "the woman who made me, encircles you, she wishes you a peaceful night. Dream of Cathedral Windows, Plaid Mountains, Broken Stars." Even on walls, quilts are intended as cover.

I selected Grandmother's Fan for this poem, from a show I visited at the State Museum in Columbia, South Carolina. Entitled "Covering All the Angles: Geometric Design in South Carolina Quilts," this show embodied the aesthetic content of the poem, as well as the striking patterns. Surrounded by a multitude of quilts from South Carolina's history, enshrined in an aesthetically appropriate yet institutional environment, I could—like Jacobik—imagine sleeping under each one.

Marvin Bell's *Quilt, Dutch China Plate*, which acknowledges "the work of women" of earlier times, honors the spiralling beauty of a quilt. It is a meditative poem that with the repetition of "This was" and "Here is" allows the quilt to recreate itself in the mind of the reader. Because of these markers, this poem exemplifies the type of poem that helps one to "read" a quilt: "Here are the points within a circle, the circle defined by its points, the articulation of fingers."

It is fitting that the quilt that accompanies Bell's poem, Resident Plate (Dresden Plate Variant), was constructed across the years by a women's class at Athens Methodist Church in Illinois. The top was constructed in 1943 and the quilting completed in 1980. In this variation of the Dresden Plate, the plates become flowers and the design keeps the eyes moving in much the way Bell's words keeps the reader's eyes moving on the imaginary quilt.

Not all encounters with quilts bring delight or reverence for the quilters. Michael McFee's *Cold Quilt*, which begins with a mention of a visit to a museum, offers a pungent interpretation of quilts that focuses not on sentimentality but on the hardship that must be threaded into so many quilts. While some poets sentimentalize the hardship, McFee comments on how quilts so often feel cold and ponders, "I wonder if it isn't the enduring dowry of bitterness stitched into them that makes us shiver."

Log Cabin, Barn Raising Arrangement embodies both the elegance of a museum piece and a stark design that might have inspired a writer to think of coldness of heart. It was constructed by an unknown quiltmaker in Lewisburg, Pennsylvania, in the late nineteenth century.

Some quilts are discovered not in family homes, quilt shows, or museums. *The Quilt* by Larry Levis is about the finding of a quilt on a trip through Pennsylvania, a quilt constructed by a woman "who must be dead now." In this poem, the narrator muses about the past embodied in this quilt found by his companion and celebrates the woman who added one bright corner of yellow to her drab quilt. The poem's opening line, however, tells us that the poem is about death as much as about the quilt. The quilt adds lightness and hope.

Levis writes, "It reminded me of laughter, of you. And some woman, Whose faith in the goodness of the world was Stubborn, sewed in."

Hole in the Barn Door Variation, an Amish quilt from 1942, selected to go with Levis' poem, also weaves light and dark, with the lightness indicative of a glimpse of sun from a hole in a barn door. The color yellow and the opening line of Levis' poem inspired this selection: "I think it is all light at the end; I think it is air." These lines may remind the reader of Bruchac's image of light through a mouse-eaten quilt.

Another poem that uses quilts as a backdrop to philosophical probing is Dina von Zweck's *Japanese Quilt*, in which the narrator spies the quilt hanging "on a wall at Tokyo Bank." This poem is based on the idea of transformation and the component of thrift seen in many of the poems. In this case, the poet begins with the image of a quilt with "strips of earth colors and veiny prints" to move into a fantasy evoked by the "second use of scraps." The quilt evokes the "beauty of old kimonos pieced by schoolgirls in Tokyo." Seeing within the patches the beauty of old cloth, the narrator states, "I catch a glimpse of what it means to be transformed."

Fuchsia was made by Kumiko Sudo, a Japanese artist who has made the United States her home. This quilt demonstrates Kumiko's unique interpretation of the traditional Japanese arts of sashiko and origami.

Another poem of this nature is about a woman contemplating the purchase of an old quilt from a woman from Missouri. *Forgiveness* by Susan Terris depicts the beauty of this pattern

"at once, exuberant, contained, a triangulated flow of motion" and also stained. The narrator cannot bring herself to buy the quilt and yet she is mesmerized by the stain, a stain which gives the quilt character as the narrator imagines the origin of the stain.

Appropriately, Ocean Waves is attributed to Mariah Potter Anderson from Webb City, Missouri, circa 1920. The undulating nature of this design is especially magnified in this quilt with its different patterns comprising the waves. This is a quilt the narrator of *Forgiveness* would buy.

While Levis and von Zweck use the quilt as a point of departure for musings about death and the meaning of life, Paul Grant's *Quilts* was written to acknowledge the finality of death. Similar to other poems, such as Corey's, that catalog of quilt names, it addresses the great variety of quilts made for the NAMES Project, which memorializes persons lost to AIDS. The litany of quilt patterns mirrors a litany of goodbyes. "The sky's as full of secrets as the earth is full of bones," writes Grant.

There is a long tradition of constructing quilts as memorials for the dead. Kentucky Graveyard Quilt, Star of Lemoine with a Border of Coffins, paired with Grant's poem, is intended to show the heritage of tombstone quilts that serve the dead. Made by Elizabeth Roseberry Mitchell in Lewis County, Kentucky, 1839, this quilt presents visual elements of the macabre evoked in words by Grant.

Some poems depict the actual use of quilts. In these, the quilt acts as more than a cover. It embodies feelings toward family, children, self, love, even death. Martha Christina's

16

Crib Notes, for example, is a love poem to a child lying under a quilt made by his mother. It philosophizes in a second-person address to the child: "Is history all perspective? You put on these patches oblivious to the past bled from them with each washing, wear them like a mantle to see you through night fears." The personal history evoked by patches from the mother's past is lost on the child, who has no consciousness of the mother's old clothes or even his own yet.

This acknowledgment of how the history of a quilt's pieces may be lost as it becomes removed from its origins is especially evident in Crib Quilt, Block Pattern, a frayed yet lovely quilt by an unknown quiltmaker from Southington, Connecticut, circa 1860. The use that the quilt clearly has weathered is contrasted with the meticulous block pattern that offers almost an optical illusion.

Under the Baby Blanket by May Swenson also addresses someone under a quilt, dubbed a "baby blanket" because it was made by a mother while awaiting the birth of her child. The play on words refers both to the use of the quilt and to its design, with "12 identical sunbonneted little girls, one in each square." In this poem, there is some conflict between the narrator—who wants to hang the quilt, "a work of art"—and the woman whose mother made it, who ends curled up on the couch asleep, a child again under the quilt her mother stitched 47 years before while expecting her (or, the narrator muses, him). The difference of opinion about the quilt parallels differences within the relationship.

In Swenson's poem, the girls are all doing something different. In the accompanying Dutch Doll/Sunbonnet Sues from the Sikes family of Tuscaloosa, Alabama, 1940, the girls are simply dressed differently. Both poem and quilt attest to the work that goes into such a quilt. "It had to take months, looks like," says the narrator of the Swenson poem to the woman who ends up asleep under it.

For her narrator to describe what it is like to sleep under her *Crazy Quilt*, Elizabeth Spires uses the random embroidery of the crazy quilt as a metaphor for the narrator's state of mind and the quilt itself as a vessel of her personal history: "Each night, eyes clothed, I walk the crazy rows: no up or down, no north or south to guide me, I zigzag, dizzy and drunk, my heart, like the quilt's, off-center." Naming the elements contrasts with the way Bell names the elements of his Quilt, Dutch China Plate, as the narrator is led by the imagery of the Crazy Quilt to walk in circles.

Spires' poem includes the sort of embroidered images of the crazy quilt illustrated in the 1885 Crazy Quilt, as well as the formal lack of symmetry. In this quilt from Virginia, made by Kate Harrison Poe in 1885, look for the horse, the pansy, and the butterfly, but also for the "road/leading through unreasoning, moonlit fields" that Spires describes.

Roberta Hill Whiteman's *Star Quilt* imagines two lovers under a quilt, one speaking to the other. It offers a prayer: "Star quilt, sewn from dawn light by fingers of flint, take away those touches meant for noisier skins, anoint us with grass and twilight air." The power of this poem lies in its message of love equally given and returned.

The Star Quilt, honored in this poem and illustrated by Evelyn Douville's quilt from the Rosebud Indian Reservation in South Dakota, 1985–86, embodies a mythological symbol of the Native American. The star motif of hide paintings and clothing of the Plains is a favorite among Native Americans who adopted quilting techniques from settlers and made them their own, in much the same way African Americans fused African imagery with colonial quilting techniques.

The Century Quilt by Marilyn Nelson Waniek was written to celebrate a family quilt made by Mary Elizabeth Thomas. "Now I've found a quilt I'd like to die under," says the narrator of Waniek's poem after describing the Indian blanket she revered as a child. Giving it the new name of The Century Quilt, the narrator extends the tradition of naming in quilt poems and weaves in her family's personal history.

The poem in this case describes the actual quilt. The brown, white, and "yellowbrown" squares each hold a "sweet gum leaf whose fingers I imagine would caress me into the silence," states the narrator. Sweet Gum Leaf that illustrates the poem with its striking, artful design is from the household of the poet. It is a quilt that is lovingly and thoughtfully used, as quilts are meant to be used.

As a whole, the poems reinforce the attributes of quilts. Just as the quilts extend the poems by aiding visualization, the poems give words to the texture and colors and themes of the quilts. The poems and quilts that follow suggest that quilters are poets, and poets are quilters.

19

A Quilt is a Gift

A quilt is a gift, whether it is one made from the heart and given to family or friend, or sold through a raffle to benefit a senior citizens' center, or bought in an estate sale or flea market. A quilt is a gift even if it hangs in a museum and is not to be touched, except perhaps by white-gloved hands. Owning a quilt is like owning the hours the quilter spent piecing and stitching. Especially today, when so much is so readily available so quickly and effortlessly, a quilt becomes a reminder that we need to remember why so many generations and groups of people have kept up the tradition.

A quilt has a language all its own. Just as a poem provides imagery that awakens our visual senses, a quilt makes words out of hexagons and squares and circles and flowers. What do these words say? They whisper or shout, affirm or remind. You can read the history of families and towns in quilts. You can read changes in the quilts that signal cultural influences and interference and accommodation. You can read about economic conditions, which are written not only in the recycled strips of cloth in some but also in the lush needlework of other quilts. Most of all, you can read affirmation of life, even in quilts made for death.

And, just as you can read a quilt, you can read and enjoy this collection of poems. My two loves—poetry and quilts— are here combined in *Words & Quilts*, the grandest of my creations so far.

21

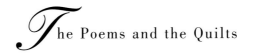

The Poems and the Quilts

QUILT, DUTCH CHINA PLATE

*T*his was sanity—of star and snowflake,

grateful for scraps and thread and bits of dust

from under the bed. Thank you for needles.

This was the prairie place the wind could not pass through

looking for a lap, the compass that pointed to home.

Here are the points within a circle, the circle

defined by its points, the articulations of fingers.

And here, wordless, are the stops between the points,

the circles inside a ring, and the copycat's square.

Here is the pinwheel, the medicine wheel, the coin as art.

Here is the wagon wheel, the train, the miles, the Midwest.

The sun is here, spinning. The eye, too, is set spinning.

These are the propellers, the fans, the slight twisting on its

axis of the pie and the plate and the bucket

whenever one was set down for a moment. This is time frozen

and the work of women. Here is how long

the absolute *now* is, the dilemma of steadfastness,

not pretty. The invisible repeats itself—

manifest sunflowers, the moon in the water.

What is to be done with such an object,

which says beautifully that design is the motion a shape makes?

—while petals bloom in the brain, and the blood

bursts to break things high overhead.

MARVIN BELL

RESIDENT PLATE
(DRESDEN PLATE VARIANT)

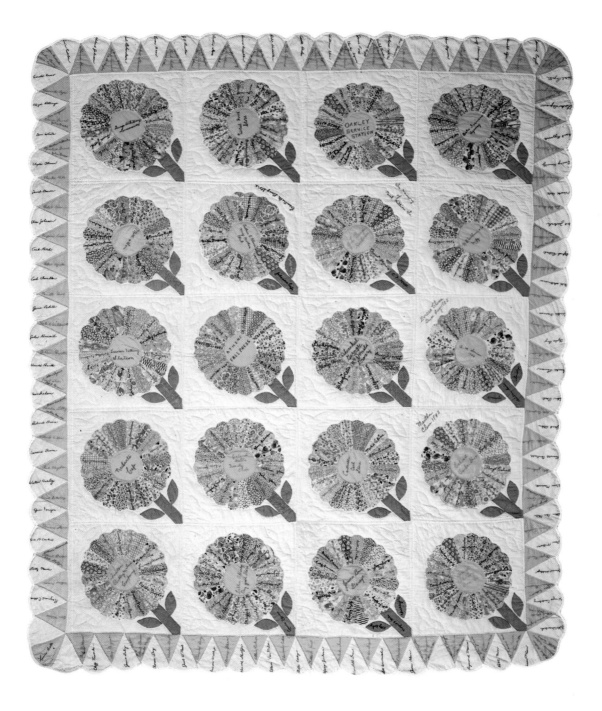

MARTHA CLASS, ATHENS METHODIST CHURCH

Athens, Illinois, 1943 (top) and 1980 (quilting)
96" × 80". Cotton.
Private Collection
Courtesy of Illinois Quilt Project, Early American Museum, Mahomet, Illinois
Photography by Will Zehr

*T*he pattern was "spider web"—
scraps of fabric forming hexagons,
their paisleys, dots and plaids
repeated until the shapes stopped,
some incomplete, at the edge,
and over the whole a web, quilted,
seven stitches to the inch drawing each corner
to the center.

In the patchwork I recognized pieces
of my grandmother's gingham apron,
the apron itself cut from the skirt
of a faded dress. Her family's clothes,
the work of her hands, for years
were conserved. Winters passed to the scrape
of scissors trimming those rectangles.

I trimmed a scrap of fabric from my old sundress,
appliqued it over the threadbare original,
bright red against worn calico.
I laid on the design by drawing needle
across fabric, quilting the impression
that would disappear like the needle's imprints
in my fingers. My stitches met hers
and I knotted the thread of this net
that would catch another generation of small hands,
clenching in sleep and letting go.

DEBORAH BROWNING

IDA JACOBS

El Dorado, Arkansas/Los Angeles, California, ca. 1950s
79-½" × 78". Cotton.
Collection of Eli Leon
Photography by Sharon Risedorph

28

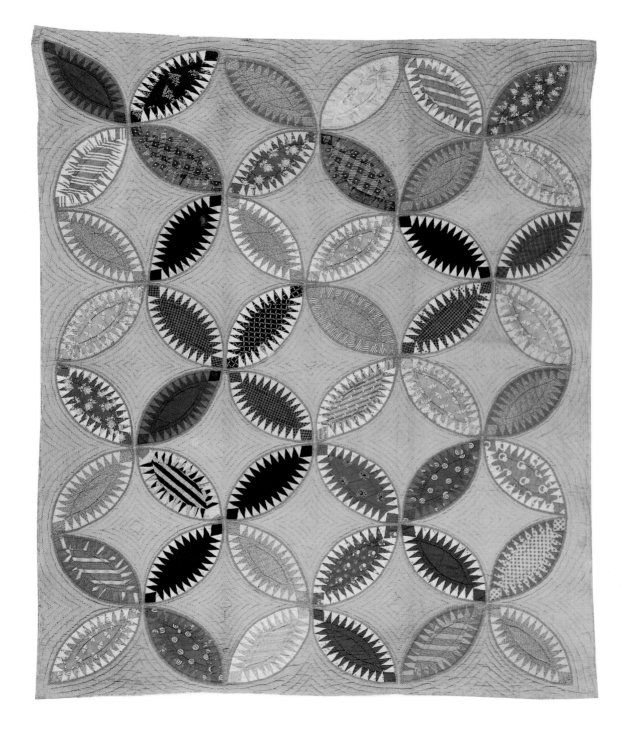

MARY NORVELL GUERRANT

Buckingham County, Virginia, ca. 1895
71" × 88". Printed and Plain Cottons.
Courtesy of the Valentine Museum, Richmond, Virginia
Photography by Katherine Wetzel
63.22

WALKING IN NOVEMBER ACROSS THE STREAM TO THE SWEAT LODGE

IN MEMORY OF SAM RAY

The leaves fallen
from the creekside maples,
no longer blaze as red as embers.

Earth brown, they close
like fists around
their own lives,
loosening into soil.

My red dog grabs a stick in her mouth,
so long it knocks against the trees
as she runs up the narrow path,
making a music which startles, delights her.

No great issues this morning,
no more to do than burn tobacco,
speak words by the fire pit,
strip the blankets from the sweat lodge.

One old quilt has become as thin as paper.
I laugh as I lift it—the white-footed mice
have stolen the batting to weave into nests.
Light shines through its patterns
of red and orange, a sudden flower.

Walking back, the wind against my face,
I am suddenly wreathed in clouds of breath.

There is no way to count
the blessings of seasons,
the fallen leaves.

JOSEPH BRUCHAC

CRIB NOTES
FOR ADAM

You say you want
to be four forever, little resister,
never to outgrow
the cage of crib, my lap,
your father's arms.

Already your feet reach out below
the hem of your patchwork quilt
where I read my history
over the soft rise and fall
of your shoulders.

The plaid of my favorite maternity dress,
bright blues washed away like pain
the body remembers, but can't recall.

Further back in that amnesia
the candy stripes of a pinafore.
I'm six; I smooth its hem and my dog
runs rabid into the neighbor's
yard, into the cross hairs
of the waiting gun.

Is history all perspective?
You put on these patches
oblivious to the past bled from them
with each washing, wear them like a mantle
to see you through night fears.

Curled again,
small cashew, deeper in sleep,
you suck your thumb,
rock rhythmically. I imagine
you imagine yourself
back in the womb,
your own history
under construction
in the patchwork of cells
that divides, divides and divides us.

MARTHA CHRISTINA

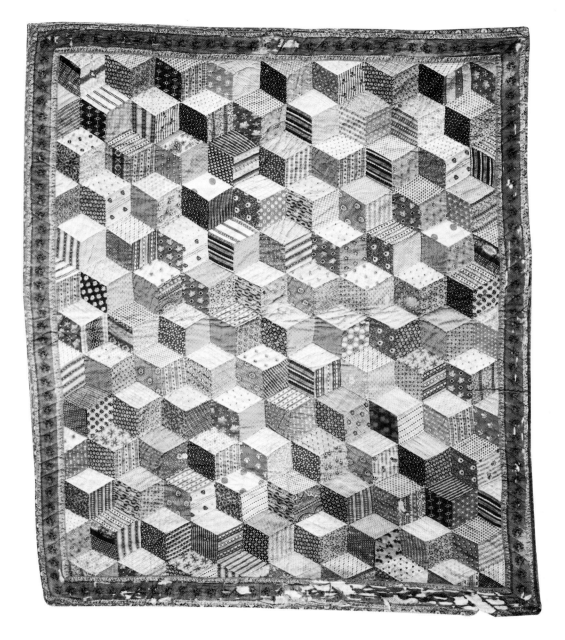

UNKNOWN QUILTMAKER

Southington, Connecticut, ca. 1860
47" × 39-¾". Cotton.
Courtesy of the Smithsonian Institution, Washington, D.C.
73-8577

MORNING CHORE
FOR CYNTHIA

They said to quit my tears and get on with the spinning.
I wince seeing mother's quilt on the chair's back,
its trees of life all bent while threads sadden
in the pot by the fire and my hands twist flax.
"Someone tell this child her grieving time is done.
Tell her there's a hard winter coming, Lord knows."
I spit and twist to a memory of leaf showers,
mother flinging me into hills of gold and following
headlong to rise, her laughter bounding past fences
that mark off the wild, hair crazy with leaves,
the leaves of a quilt that covers me at night,
covers my secret body that goes on sprouting
though my heart desists as wheels of sleep
spin stars and plumes, lilies, thistles, cat tracks:
emblems of wonder frozen at my waking.

SUZANNE UNDERWOOD CLARK

IORA ALMINA PHILO POOL

Sunbright, Morgan County, Tennessee, 1870
83" × 75-½". Cotton.
Collection of Betty Holman Pickett and Gwen Holman Kelly
Courtesy of "The Quilts of Tennessee"

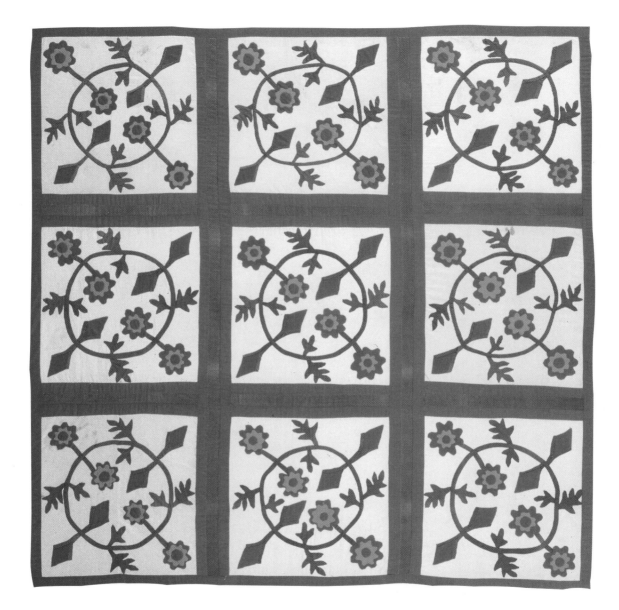

34

LEYENDECKER FAMILY

Columbus, Texas, ca. 1890
76" × 76". Cotton Percale and Muslin.
Courtesy of The Witte Museum, San Antonio,
and The San Antonio Museum Association, Texas
73.122(4)

QUILTS

One woman wept, they say,
when a peddler reached her cabin
with no new patterns to sell.

Irish Chain, Persian Pear, Rose of Tennessee

I still make my bed with *Kansas Troubles*—
I was only five when Mother said,
"Twelve you must have in your hope chest, before
the Bridal Quilt, and that before you'll wed."
First my stitches tried to mirror hers,
our hands touching as we worked.
At night she plucked mine out
to keep her project whole.
Next came simple sewings: double lines
and scallops on my own crazy quilt.

Bear Track, Turkey Track, Beauty of Kaintuck

Some days, when Tommy and Jimmy ran outside
shouting off the chickens, I thought
I'd stretched myself across that frame, waiting
for the womenfolk to pad and quilt and bind me.
Yet with all the years of work,

when the time came Joseph had to wait
seven months while I finished *Jacob's Tears.*
The Bridal must be perfect, Mother warned.
A broken thread, a crop gone bad;
a twisted stitch, a baby dead.

Wreath of Grapes, Flying Swallows, Pomegranate Tree

Sometimes our life is no more than the names we give:
Joseph moved us to Missouri,
and the women loved my *Jacob's Tears*—
but they knew it as *The Slave Chain.*
In the Texas flatland winds, *Texas Tears*
lay across the bed, and after the last move
we slept warm beneath *The Road to Kansas.*
That was many droughts and storms ago.
The colors still blaze enough to shame
a Puritan, and not a seam has given way.
Joseph is gone, but even coldest nights
my *Kansas Troubles* brings me through till Dawn.

35

STEPHEN COREY

QUILTING

*W*e sit at the frame,
three women backstitching
eight stitches to an inch
the way our grandmother
taught us. Alternating
triangles of "Heaven and Earth"
reflect and shadow afternoon sun
and the radio plays softly as we
talk about the yellow material
from Alice's skirt and how it looks
next to the dark blue with roses.

Soon we will straighten fingers
just beginning to gnarl,
stretch our backs and go home
to fix supper for the husbands
we married thirty years ago.

But not for a while.

The sun gathers golden
in my sister's parlor and
dust motes sparkle in the
slanting light. Dishwashers,
grown children, and darkness
seem far away. We place
the triangles together
as we have done so often
and stitch, thimbles blinking
light across the pattern.

ANNE GEORGE

FOUR PATCH AND
TRIANGLES COMBINATION

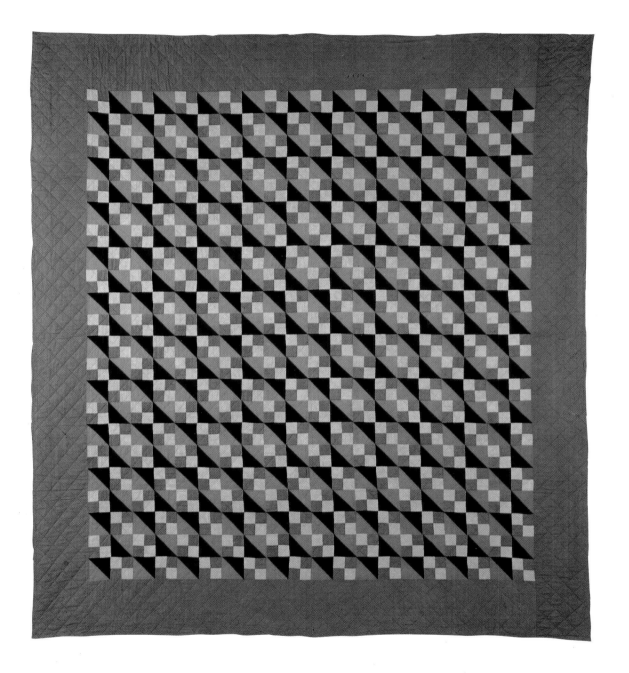

37

BARBARA ZOOK PEACHEY

Mifflin County, Pennsylvania, ca. 1910
84" × 78". Cotton.
Collection of the Museum of American Folk Art, New York
Gift of Mr. and Mrs. William B. Wigton
1984.24.12

QUILTS

Star of the Heart, Mexican Star.

We dream old women around a hanging
frame in the dance hall of ancestors.
Through them we patch the sky.

Lifted Star, Rolling Star.
I camp alone in river country, gone
to ground from traveling around with the blues,
shivering to October's careless touch.

O, *Carolina Lily.* O, *Baltimore Bouquet.*
The sky's as full of secrets as the earth
is full of bones, and when the moon
goes down, my own come up, come clean:
Rainheart and *Spidersbreath, October Cave*
and, before sleep, *The Hemlock Laughing.*

Prairie Star, Log Cabin Star.
Our savings as they dwindle grow
together in a patchwork argument
warm to the touch, to the memory.

Star of Lemoine with a Border of Coffins.
Marching across the night, between the glow
of the guttering campfire and the sky,
the crazy names parade off their grandmother-maze,
one-of-a-kind and kindly singing
me awake with its shape-note certainty
to see them disappear into the river, calling
Southern Double-Cross, Lion's Share,
See You on the Other Side.

PAUL GRANT

KENTUCKY GRAVEYARD QUILT
STAR OF LEMOINE WITH A
BORDER OF COFFINS

ELIZABETH ROSEBERRY MITCHELL

Lewis County, Kentucky, 1839
85" x 81". Cotton.
Collection of the Kentucky Historical Society
Louisville, Kentucky

40

ELLEN NELSON PEARSON

Princeton, Illinois, 1910
70" × 67".
Collection of Pamela J. Cain
Courtesy of Illinois Quilt Project, Early American Museum, Mahomet, Illinois
Photography by Will Zehr

PATCHWORK

From the scrap barrel at work I pilfered scraps—
rags, ends of bolts. Grandmother jerked
thread through the cloth so hard the batting bulged.
We fought for those crude quilts, me and my brothers.
She yanked the stitches till they puckered, and slowly
the stolen scraps yielded a Drunkard's Path.

Grandmomma's ten-years dead and her bad work
still keeps me hot at night, in Northern weather,
which she despised, just as she hated you
if you are Northern, rich, black, smart, or atheist.
I loved her because, like God, she loved me first,
ferociously. A love so close to hate
it's taken decades just to say there is a difference.

I sat between her knees, head tilted back.
She thumbed the crusty threads. "There ain't no call
to pay some doctor to do this." She snipped
the threads lacing my forehead, popped them out.
But first she studied them and said, "It's sloppy—
these big loose stitches. I'd sew you tighter." She grinned,
and with a lipless peck she kissed the stitches.

ANDREW HUDGINS

THE QUILT SHOW

*A*mong these lozenges, rhomboids and octagons
of cotton, love is bound by Double-Wedding Rings,
the heavens brightened with Feathered Stars.

Like mazes or puzzles or Goldbach's conjectures,
intelligence flowers, seeks in pleasing patterns
and colors, an underlying order, a true design.

Grandmother's Fans cool wrinkled faces
while the young are tied in Lover's Knots.
Alone, in odd hours, through the long months,

a woman sews zigzag, sawtooth or parallel stitches,
or secures the cotton waddling in concentric
circles; life within a life, child within a womb.

On its frame, the quilt spreads, a globe wrapped
in Double-Irish Chains, or in gradual shades
light steps-down through squares of Tumbling Blocks.

Beside a Log Cabin, or a Yankee Puzzle, Cottage Tulips
bloom. A quilt on the bed says: *the woman who made me,*
encircles you, she wishes you a peaceful night. Dream
of Cathedral Windows, Plaid Mountains, Broken Stars.

GRAY JACOBIK

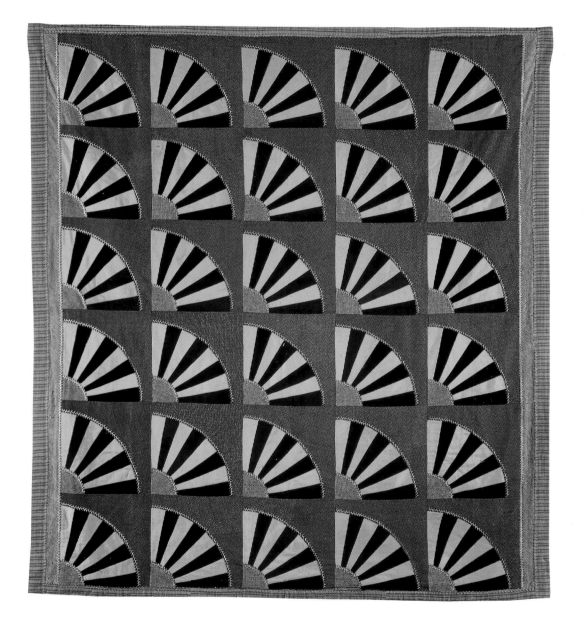

43

Lexington County, South Carolina, ca. 1900
78" × 72". Wool and Cotton.
Collection of the Lexington County Museum, Lexington, South Carolina

QUILT SUTRA:
"UNDERGROUND RAILROAD"
EARLY 1800s

*N*o forsythia scraps
to emblazon spring. No
wedding ring pattern,
but headache blues, bone-
splitting indigo patches;
slats of bruise yellow
zigzagged on, stem-
stitched like Hokusai
waves to the underside
of outside compliance

so that—tacked down
between scalded jam
jars, between spooning
scum, boiling bones,
and straining broth, or
in hours gathered up
into industrious chatty
bees, puckers of folded
sun, hooped petticoats—
a mind could hang fire

under it, catch itself
in missionary position,
in a runaway thought:
Abolition!
so the visual metaphor
would chafe the heart
warmed under it, so
(Sarah Grimké said)
wherever needle entered
the muslin parlors—pie
wedges of flour-white
sheeting for "safe houses"
pieced against hickory
bark browns, sunflower
eye umbers—and slipped
out along the worn cotton
"lines," a slave owner's
conscience might be pricked
and a shred of gospel
respect bleed through.

SUSAN KELLY-DEWITT

YVONNE WELLS

Tuscaloosa, Alabama, 1989
62" × 82". Rayon (Found Quilt Top) and Cotton (Narrative).
Collection of Sandra McPherson
Photography by Sam Woo

HOLE IN THE BARN
DOOR VARIATION

THE QUILT

"He had stopped believing in the
goodness of the world."

Henry James, *The Portrait of a Lady*

*T*think it is all light and at the end; I think it is air.
Those fields we drove past, turning to mud in April,
Those oaks with snow still roosting in them. Towns so small
Their entire economy suffered if a boy, late at night,
Stole the bar's only cue ball.

In one of them, you bought an old quilt, which, fraying,
Still seemed to hold the sun, especially in one
Bright corner, made from what they had available in yellow
In 1897. It reminded me of laughter, of you. And some woman,
Whose faith in the goodness of the world was
Stubborn, sewed it in. "There now," she might as well
Have said, as if in answer to the snow, which was

Merciless. "There now," she seemed to say, to
Both of us. "Here's this patch of yellow. One field gone
Entirely into light. Goodbye…" We had become such artists
At saying goodbye; it made me wince to look at it.
Something at the edge of the mouth, something familiar
That makes the mouth turn down. An adjustment.

It made me wince to have to agree with her there, too,
To say the day itself, the fields, each thread

She had to sew in the poor light of 1897,
Were simply gifts. Because she must be dead by now, &
Anonymous, I think she had a birthmark on her cheek;
And if she outlived one dull husband, I think she
Still grew, out of spite & habit, flowers to give away.

If laughter is adult, an adjustment to loss,
I think she could laugh at the worst. When I think of you both,

I think of that one square of light in her quilt,
Of women, stubborn, believing in the goodness of the world.
How next year, driving past this place which I have seen
For years, & steadily, through the worst weather, when
The black of the Amish buggies makes the snow seem whiter,
I won't even have to look up.
I will wince & agree with you both, &, past the farms
Abandoned to moonlight, past one late fire burning beside
A field, the flame rising up against the night
To take its one solitary breath, even I
will be a believer.

LARRY LEVIS

WRITTEN ON THE BACK OF A LAURENS COUNTY MAP

On the tender spring grass of the back lawn
Mother and I have laid the freshly washed quilts.
Muslin, brown and green, dyed from roots
we've forgotten how to use—if we ever knew.
Colors of summer dresses, a favorite
work shirt, Easter clothes worn to piecework now.
Patterns dance out across the yard into
the flower borders and tomato vines—Drunkard's
Path, Road to Dublin, Triple Irish Chain,
Log Cabin, Lone Star. The greening grass
and warm sun bleach the stains of four generations.
We all lie there. My mother, my grandmother Tid,
Aunt Elisa, Great Grandmother Mary Belle who is
still beautiful beyond memory. Her sisters,
Mama Juliet with daughters Tannie and Book,
spinsters to this day—and Gertrude,
who married Jack when Mary Belle died young.
If he'd stayed on the railroad, we'd find
cousins spread the length of the state.
They are all here, spines religiously straight,
doing piecework from the same basket.

Then they lie down, we all lie down
on our stomachs, our sides, tossing the high
topped ladies' shoes aside and looking up
through a canopy of green leaves. They are
talking. They are talking of nothing,
nothing in particular—memories proud
and sorrowful stitched into rows, edges turned
and tied down. The branches above us wide
and alive, alive with the greening up of each
moment, of clean linens bleaching in the sun.
They seem very near, each willow oak leaf separate
and complete, rustling its voice in the breeze.
All of my people, bodies larger than mine,
the dead ones growing more shadowy and distinct
with time. All of my people lying on quilts
in the sun, somehow all on this earth,
on the grass, in the summer morning.
They draw me in, show me the careful
stitches, fine and straight. Hold me with them
as one who belongs, familiar in this place.
Hold me to them, but they will not ever,
no, not now, not ever, tell me who I am.

ELIZABETH H. McDADE

49

ELIZA HUGER

Anderson County, South Carolina, ca. 1845
107" × 106". Cotton.
Courtesy of the Charleston Museum, Charleston, South Carolina

COLD QUILT

*O*ur clear-eyed guide said it is the slick
cotton that makes quilts cold. I wonder
if it isn't the enduring dowry of bitterness
stitched into them that makes us shiver,
as in that quilt (unfit for hanging) handed
down to me from my father's mother, begun
the day her husband died, a lifelong lament

composed of old suits and shirts he'd worn,
threaded to her leftover dresses, its design—
each pane a basket of memorial flowers,
a dozen loud triangles tipped on their sides—
a stiff pastiche of grief and the solitary
nights spent trying to transform their bad luck
into something useful, used. No busy bee

touched that quilt. Her life became a patchwork
of quilted plenty, her yard a dormitory
of vegetable beds, her table a dazzling pattern
of cakes and pies. But she stayed skinny
and wrapped herself in the plain handmade cocoon
of that death-quilt every night, even when
she began to fade in her children's used beds.

At the funeral home, my uncle the soldier
draped her coffin with it, prayed, then handed
her life's flag to me, compactly folded, her
crooked stitches and nearly-rotten panes still
tenacious after half a century, the sheep
I count now in the inherited dark, her cold quilt
a poultice I spread on my chest before sleep.

MICHAEL MCFEE

LOG CABIN, BARN RAISING
ARRANGEMENT

UNKNOWN QUILTMAKER

Lewisburg, Pennsylvania, late 19th century
68" × 68". Silk.
Courtesy of the Smithsonian Institution, Washington, D.C.
76-2663

52

KATHY MARX

Nolensville, Tennessee, 1992
47" × 75". Cotton and Lamé.
Collection of the Artist
Photo courtesy of Chromatics, Inc.

ANNABELLE CAIN MCMILLAN
GRANDMOTHER

Your first name a softness, like wildflowers

pressed at a book's secret center,

but by the time of my father's birth, that softness

was tempered to a cutting edge

through years of tilling soil as forbidding as a curse.

You hold a short chain of memories: the son

who graduated from high school and joined the navy,

the threadbare clothing and flour sacks

you pieced into coverlets

quilted by a roomful of women in just one day.

You do not hear that same son

repeat bitter stories of childhood,

crops parched to paper from drought, dirt floors,

wells that again and again ran dry,

do not know that I think of you when I turn to my sewing:

pillowslips embroidered with roses, quilts

made from lengths of bright purchased fabric.

I take the small cold steel of a needle in my hand,

stitch patterns your life would not let you imagine.

JOAN MCMILLAN

QUILT TOP DISCOVERED AT THE MUSKOGEE FLEA MARKET AND FOUND TO CONTAIN BLOCKS RESEMBLING CERTAIN DESIGNS OF DESCENDANTS OF MAROONS IN SURINAME

*B*rief, direct stitches, wild eye.
Her knots still eddy
from finger-winding, pulling.

Unblending plaid compilations, like gourd heaps
or melon stripes rolled into a mound,
poppy and tansy-yellow squashes, striated cucumbers, leanings
of December cornstalks still offering
late, secret usefulness.

She measured nothing. But she used
all notions of rough equality
to scissor the unlike prints similar,
then sewed them back together to clash.

In Suriname the Saramaka gossips named
their cloth: *blackbird fat* (for orange lines),
okra water (dark and steaming), *co-wife
peppered co-wife* (pink in honor
of the one who crushed hot chilis
into her co-wife's douche).

And the lowdown condenses,
candid, in these Oklahoma squares:
a handkerchief-sized closetful
of fifty brights, none so small
it can't tell how her comfort
liked to move in it.

So she is glad she told herself this way.

And this: a handwriting
of close, irreproachable stitches
tells her, from the back.

SANDRA MCPHERSON

QUILT TOP
FOUND IN MUSKOGEE, OKLAHOMA

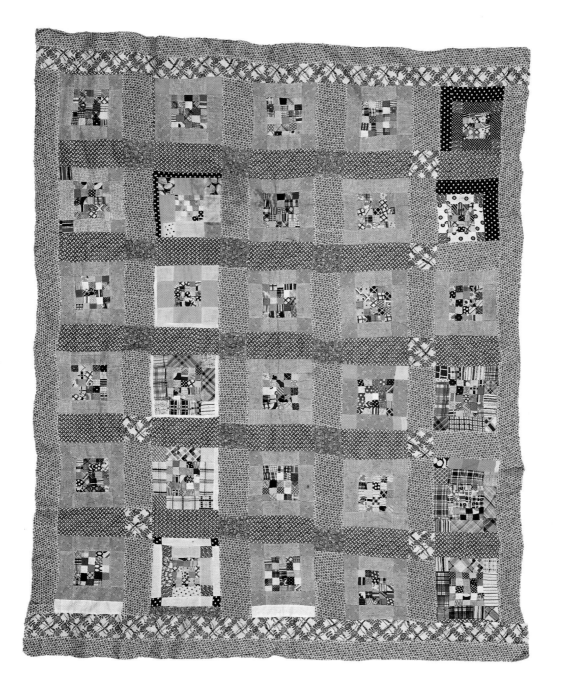

UNKNOWN QUILTMAKER

Muskogee, Oklahoma, ca. 1930
76" × 81". Cotton.
Collection of Sandra McPherson
Photography by Sam Woo

HOW TO READ A QUILT

*S*tand back and note geometry of line,

get a feel for angles and corners

as you comprehend symmetry, asymmetry.

Scan patterns of color, the top, the bottom,

the way small pieces fold into a fit.

Read from edge to center, diagonally,

horizontally, in circles and backwards,

till your mind is captured by small print

and you stand closer to decipher the quilting.

Swirls, hearts, octagons, triangles—

and more, the alphabet hieroglyphic.

There is no syntax, only the meaning each

combination of cloth, thread, and needle yields.

An hourglass becomes a martingale;

an embroidered semi-circle, the moon.

The unsighted can read with deft fingers,

make out a message with a sweeping touch

to feel a knot or silk, wool, cotton,

the way the pieces merge and emerge.

Themes connect and transform as

families are united, children born,

the dead saluted and put to rest.

Everyone can read between the lines

the promise of warm nights, clear mornings.

FELICIA MITCHELL

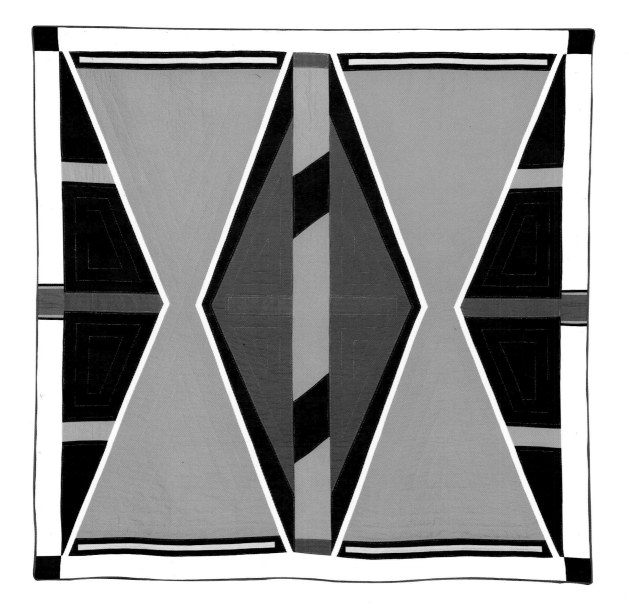

57

MARGARET WOOD

Seminole/Navajo, Florida, 1984
89-⅛" × 89-⅛". Cotton.
Courtesy of the Heard Museum, Phoenix, Arizona
Photography by Craig Smith

58

KATE HARRISON POE

Virginia, 1885
80-½" × 62". Silks and Velvet, Embroidery.
Courtesy of The Valentine Museum, Richmond, Virginia
Photography by Katherine Wetzel
80-134

CRAZY QUILT

Each night, eyes closed, I walk the crazy rows:
no up or down, no north or south
to guide me, I zigzag, dizzy and drunk,
my heart, like the quilt's, off-center.

The sun and moon, at odds with one another,
shine darkly from different corners.
Random stars point this way and that.
A dog barks. A calico cat meows.
An owl hoots, not unkindly, "Who? Who?
Who are you looking for?"
Before I can answer, it disappears.

A house, a heart, a tree.
This must be childhood, a road
leading through unreasoning, moonlit fields
I almost remember. The only rule is simple:
for each step forward, take one step back.

I find a piece of silk from my mother's
wedding dress, still gleaming whitely,
a tie my father used to wear.
Each thing I touch initialled and pieced-in
carefully, my birth, a wedding anniversary.
But something's always missing.
"Not for a child's ears," they said
when I asked, "Who's dead? Who disappeared?"

Each night I walk the quilt in circles,
retracing the past, waiting for morning
to call me back. "Mother, where are you?"
I call and call, my voice travelling
beyond me, echoing back. I hear her answer,
so near, so far within the quilt's
dark borders, "I'm here. I'm here."

ELIZABETH SPIRES

MOTHER'S POSTAGE
STAMP QUILT
ANNA SMITH MOHR 1907–1975

After she finished the flower garden quilt

she dared to use some of the money she saved

from selling eggs to buy a little fabric

for accents on her next one.

Scraps from her everyday sewing made

the most blocks, but around the mosaic

geometric shape of the center the colors

splashed like sunset, peachglow, embers,

burnt orange merging into night

at the black sateen around the border.

Like ladders or lightning bolts

the blazing and dark one-inch-square blocks

set off the bottle blue from her aprons,

the red-check from the twins' dresses,

applegreen from the lining of a skirt,

Mrs. Hilmer's shell pink scraps, Aunt Stena's

turquoise prints. In a house without

any pictures, this was her picture,

her quilting stitches as tiny as secrets,

pattern on pattern which only the knowing eye

could see.

ANN STRUTHERS

UNKNOWN QUILTMAKER

Ohio, ca. 1930
82" × 76". Cottons.
Robert Cargo Folk Art Gallery, Tuscaloosa, Alabama

UNDER THE BABY BLANKET

*U*nder the baby blanket 47 years old you are
asleep on the worn too-short Leatherette sofa.

Along with a watermelon and some peaches from
the beach cottage, you brought home this gift

from your Mom. "Just throw it in the van," you
said, "I haven't time to talk about it."

She had wanted to tell how she handstitched and
appliquéd the panels—a dozen of them—waiting

for you to be born: 12 identical sunbonneted
little girls, one in each square, in different

colors of dresses doing six different things.
And every tiny stitch put in with needle and

thimble. "It had to take months, looks like,"
I said. "Well, Mom's Relief Society ladies

must have helped," you said. One little girl
is sweeping, one raking, another watering a plant

in a pot, one dangling a doll dressed exactly
like herself. One is opening a blue umbrella.

At center is a little girl holding a book, with
your initial on the cover! I was astonished:

"A Matriarchal Blessing, predicting your future!"
(But, wait a minute, I thought. How did she know

you wouldn't be a boy? Was she also sewing
another blanket, with little boys in its squares:

holding hammer, riding tricycle, playing with
dog, batting ball, sailing boat, and so on?)

I asked for the baby blanket—which *is* a work
of art—to be hung on the wall above the sofa

where I could study it. You refused. You
lay down under it, bare legs drawn up, a smudge

of creosote on one knee. Almost covered with
little girls 47 years old you've gone to sleep.

MAY SWENSON

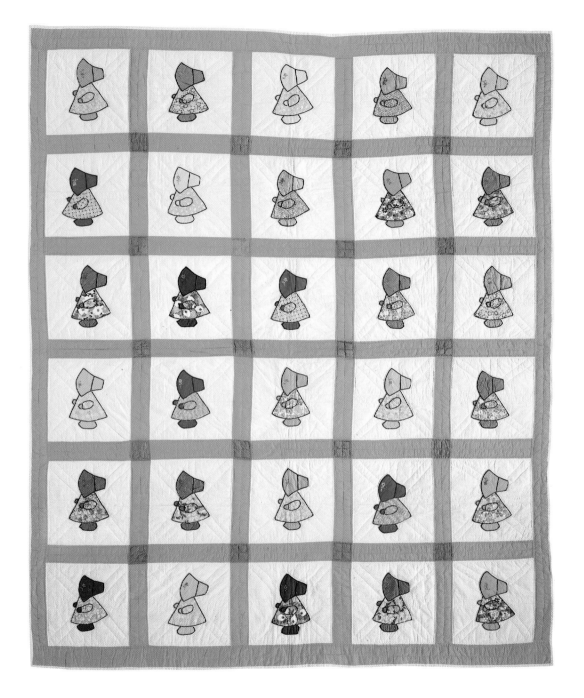

BESSIE SIKES (OR POSSIBLY HER MOTHER)

Tuscaloosa, Alabama, 1940
96" × 78". Cottons.
Robert Cargo Folk Gallery, Tuscaloosa, Alabama

64

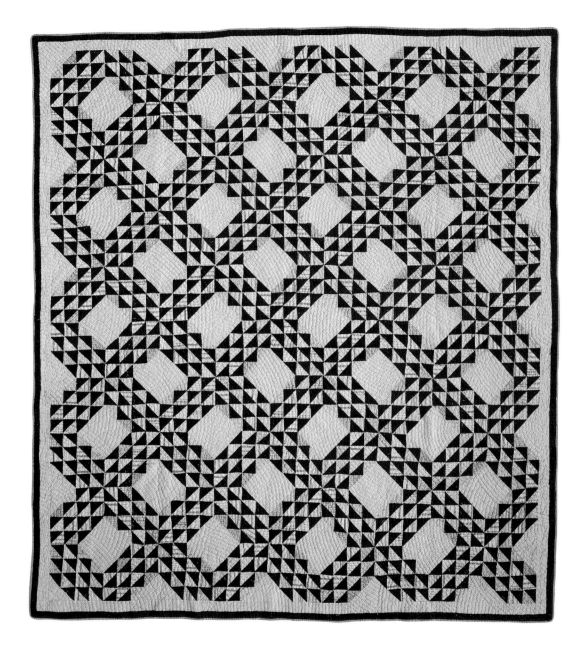

POTTER FAMILY (ATTRIBUTED TO MARIAH POTTER ANDERSON)

Webb City, Missouri, ca. 1920s
79" × 71". Cotton.
Collection of Eli Leon
Photography by Sharon Risedorph

FORGIVENESS

Sometimes, I buy old quilts but never ones
with any stain. No tea, no blood,
or fluids that will not succumb to Tide.
This work, tendered by a woman from
Missouri, is Ocean Waves, 1890—white
with hand-dipped blue—loved, necessary.

Its pattern is, at once, exuberant, contained,
a triangulated flow of motion.
Yearning, I stretch my hands; yet when we
(the woman from Missouri and I) sail
the quilt outside on her line, there—
borne on the crest of a wave—is a mark.
India ink. An exclamation point. Indelible.

The ink, I'm sure (men do not write in bed),
was dropped by a woman. Rorschached,
I stare until I see someone
who dreamed oceans and words.
I know how, propped on pillows, fingers
calloused from milking, stitch-pitted,
she scrawled. Alone at night, she stole
time to piece thoughts. But the quilt has

a stain. "No," I, sighing, tell the woman
from Missouri. Still, that erst-while quilter,
glances up from her tablet, squints
across time, summons me,
alien of the future world. I do not move.
Irked by my caution, she beckons,
gestures impatiently with her pen.
A single drop falls, leaving
a message that will last a hundred years.

"Stained," I murmur, undulated by
Ocean Waves, glancing toward the woman
from Missouri. Though she is speaking,
her words lap past me as I (questioning
whether anything of mine will last
a hundred years) hear only
the other one, the one with the pen.
Head, *hand*, *heart*, she urges. *Courage.*
Eyes salted, I nod. Then, for what we cannot
change, I forgive both her and myself.

SUSAN TERRIS

JAPANESE QUILT

*The beauty of old kimonos
pieced by schoolgirls in Tokyo*

Thin strips of earth colors and
veiny prints. A frugal second

use for scraps, hanging on
the wall at Tokyo Bank. I catch

a glimpse of what it means to
live on, transformed. Very wide

sleeves give way to ochre circles, in
my mind everything beautiful

is saved. I picture a woman rise
from the tatami and—outside,

on the moon-viewing platform—greet
the nightwind & nightflower. In

another piece of the quilt—a deep
cranberry triangle—I find

whispers & laughter in trees
and hurrying feet. It is the

Prince who pleads with her
for a song. And standing here

in a Tokyo bank, I wonder why
she does not sing? I remember

he still calls out: *In the fierce
wind, where is your song?*

It is the quilt—finally—that sings, and
the song rises like invisible

threads floating in air, high above
the customers counting out yen.

DINA VON ZWECK

K U M I K O   S U D O

Eugene, Oregon, 1994
34" × 34". Cotton.
Collection of Kumiko Sudo
Photography by Sharon Risedorph

THE QUILTERS

These are the strides we take
while children sleep.
Now we spread the white cloth.
We break open a rose petal by petal.
One hundred stitches shape
the edge of a leaf. From our
hands, a lattice of stars, hollyberries,
baskets, vines, drawn into the heavens
where they'll stay despite all
that goes on under and above them.

Patience, obedience, stillness.
The skies compose on our laps,
spun from a willingness to sit,
to know the pores of cloth,
the weave of breath that slips
from children's mouths, the breath
of galaxies, their trails
of dust already pulling together,
our heads surrounding the world
like undiscovered planets.

DOROTHY WALL

PINWHEEL, WITH STUFFED WORK

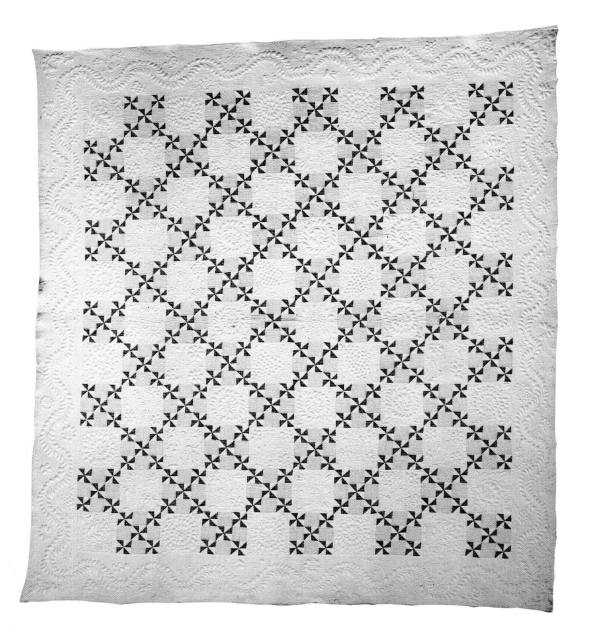

UNKNOWN QUILTMAKER

Maryland, ca. 1812
94" × 85". Cotton.
Courtesy of the Smithsonian Institution, Washington, D.C.

70

SARAH MARY TAYLOR

Yazoo City, Mississippi, ca. 1980s
74" x 68". Cotton.
Collection of Marily Nelson Waniek
Photography by Frank Noelker

THE CENTURY QUILT

FOR SARAH MARY TAYLOR, QUILTER

Marilyn Nelson Waniek

My sister and I were in love
with Meema's Indian blanket.
We fell asleep under army green
issued to Daddy by Supply.
When Meema came to live with us
she brought her medicines, her cane,
and the blanket I found on my sister's bed
the last time I visited her.
I remembered how I'd planned to inherit
that blanket, how we used to wrap ourselves
at play in its folds and be chieftains
and princesses.

Now I've found a quilt
I'd like to die under:
Six Van Dyke brown squares,
two white ones, and one square
the yellowbrown of Mama's cheeks.
Each square holds a sweet gum leaf
whose fingers I imagine
would caress me into the silence.

I think I'd have good dreams
for a hundred years under this quilt,

as Meema must have, under her blanket,
dreamed she was a girl again in Kentucky
among her yellow sisters,
their grandfather's white family
nodding at them when they met.
When their father came home from his store
they cranked up the pianola
and all of the beautiful sisters
giggled and danced.
She must have dreamed about Mama
when the dancing was over:
a lanky girl trailing after her father
through his Oklahoma field.

Perhaps under this quilt
I'd dream of myself,
of my childhood of miracles,
of my father's burnt umber pride,
my mother's ochre gentleness.
Within the dream of myself
perhaps I'd meet my son
or my other child, as yet unconceived.
I'd call it The Century Quilt,
after its pattern of leaves.

MARILYN NELSON WANIEK

PATCHWORK

She stitched little squares because she hated
throwing anything away: housedresses
and boxer shorts, scraps too gay to be dustcloths,
rescued from the ragman and reborn.

She squints at the Rose of Sharon appliqued
from her wedding dress. Her heart swells
as she clutches the sateen bouquets. Sixty years
of marriage. She scales Jacob's Ladder,
her husband's Sunday-go-to-meeting ties,
and longs to climb higher, higher, sleep
with him again. She weeps over Job's Tears—
the Slave Chain her grandmother wore
on her deathbed; links threadbare with sacrifice.
She cradles a crib-sized comforter, Tumbling Blocks
pieced from petticoats for her firstborn—
stillborn. In a gooseneck rocker she unfolds
heirlooms, linens that summered in her hope chest,
releasing scents of cedar, spirits of kinfolk.

What becomes of faith when you outlive those you love?
Patches, like hand-me-downs, wear on. Draping
her lap, a quilted geography, terrain of textures;
valleys at her fingertips and Glory beyond.
The Evening Star, frayed, is leading her home.

CAROLE BOSTON WEATHERFORD

CRAZY QUILT WITHIN CONTAINED BORDERS

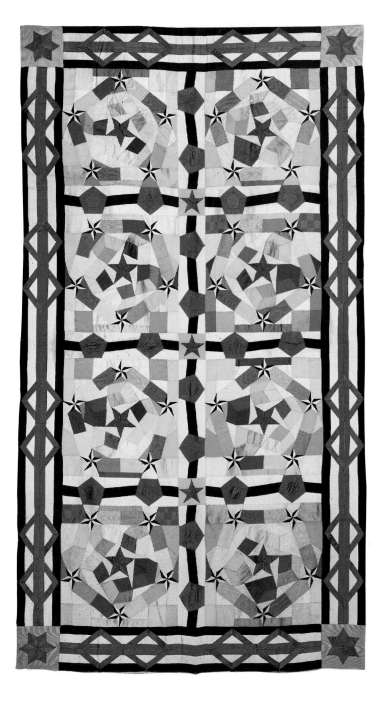

UNKNOWN QUILTMAKER

Found in New Hope, Pennsylvania, 1875–1900
81-½" × 44-½". Pieced Silk.
Collection of the Museum of American Folk Art, New York
Gift of Jacqueline L. Fowler
1981.2.1

STAR QUILT

*T*hese are notes to lightning in my bedroom.
A star forged from linen thread and patches.
Purple, yellow, red like diamond suckers, children

of the star gleam on sweaty nights. The quilt unfolds
against sheets, moving, warm clouds of Chinook.
It covers my cuts, my red birch clusters under pine.

Under it your mouth begins a legend,
and wide as the plain, I hope Wisconsin marshes
promise your caress. The candle locks

us in forest smells, your cheek tattered
by shadow. Sweetened by wings, my mothlike heart
flies nightly among geraniums.

We know of land that looks lonely,
but isn't, of beef with hides of velveteen,
of sorrow, an eddy in blood.

Star quilt, sewn from dawn light by fingers
of flint, take away those touches
meant for noisier skins,

anoint us with grass and twilight air,
so we may embrace, two bitter roots
pushing back into the dust.

ROBERTA HILL WHITEMAN

EVELYN DOUVILLE

Rosebud Indian Reservation, South Dakota, 1985–86
94" × 72".
Collection of Virginia Hunsche Randermann
Courtesy of Illinois Quilt Project
Photography by Will Zehr

CONTRIBUTORS

MARVIN BELL is the author of thirteen books. Two were published in 1994: *The Book of the Dead Man* (poems) from Copper Canyon Press and *A Marvin Bell Reader* (poems, journals, memoirs, essays) from the University Press of New England. He teaches for the Writers' Workshop at the University of Iowa and lives in Iowa City, Iowa, and Port Townsend, Washington.

DEBORAH BROWNING received her M.F.A. from Georgia State University in June 1993. Her poems have appeared in *Poem*, *Tar River Poetry*, *Kansas Quarterly*, and *Georgetown Review*.

JOSEPH (JOE) BRUCHAC is a writer and storyteller whose most recent books include a novel entitled *Dawn Land* (Fulcrum Publishing, 1993) and *Fox Song*, a children's book from Philomel (1993). He lives in the Adirondack foothills town of Greenfield Center, New York, in the same house he was raised in by his grandparents.

MARTHA CHRISTINA teaches in the Creative Writing Program at Roger Williams University where she also edits *Calliope* and directs Ampersand Press. She is the mother of two daughters and two sons; her poems have appeared in a variety of little magazines.

SUZANNE UNDERWOOD CLARK lives with her husband and three children in Bristol, Tennessee, where she homeschools, writes poetry, and teaches English part time at King College. Her poems have appeared in numerous literary magazines such as *Shenandoah*, *The Salt Creek Reader*, and *The Lullwater Review*. She is also the author of a nonfiction book, *Blackboard Blackmail*.

STEPHEN COREY has published six collections of poems, most recently *All These Lands You Call One Country* (University of Missouri Press, 1992) and *Attacking the Pieta* (State Street Press, 1988). Individually, his poems, essays, and reviews have appeared in numerous periodicals, among them *Poetry*, *The American Poetry Review*, *The Kenyon Review*, *The New Republic*, *Small Press*, and *Yellow Silk*. He co-founded (in 1977) and edited *The Devil's Millhopper*. Since 1983, he has been on the staff of *The Georgia Review*, where he is currently associate editor.

ANNE GEORGE is the author of three chapbooks of poetry. Her work has been published in many literary journals and anthologies as well as read on National Public Radio. She is the 1992–1993 recipient of an Individual Fellowship from the Alabama State Council on the Arts.

PAUL GRANT, a native of Louisiana, recently traded Washington, D.C., for Iowa City. A typographer and assemblage artist, his broadsides and boxes have appeared in several shows, and his poems have appeared in *Sewanee Review*, *Georgia Review*, *Poetry Northwest*, and numerous other periodicals. Two limited editions, *Soundtracks* (1969) and *Raw Meat And Flowers* (1981) have come out of his Gallowglass imprint, as well as the series *The Horae* (1978) of silkscreened prints—all in collaboration with other artists.

ANDREW HUDGINS is a professor of English at The University of Cincinnati. His four books of poems are *Saints and Strangers* (Houghton Mifflin, 1985), *After the Lost War* (Houghton Mifflin, 1988), *The Never–Ending* (Houghton Mifflin, 1991), and *The Glass Hammer* (Houghton Mifflin, 1994). *After the Lost War* received the Poets' Prize for 1988.

GRAY JACOBIK publishes poems in literary magazines and journals across the United States. She teaches literature and serves as Poet-in-Residence at Eastern Connecticut State University in Willimantic, Connecticut. She makes her home with her husband and several "fur-persons" in Pomfret, Connecticut. The Quilt Show that inspired

the poem that appears in this book is the annual show in Charleston, Illinois.

SUSAN KELLY-DEWITT is a poet, teacher, and painter whose poems have been published in many magazines and anthologies. She has been a Wallace Stegner Fellow at Stanford University. She is currently co-director of an arts program for homeless and disadvantaged women.

LARRY LEVIS teaches at Virginia Commonwealth University in Richmond. His most recent collection of poetry is *The Widening Spell of the Leaves* (University of Pittsburgh Press, 1991).

ELIZABETH H. MCDADE grew up in Charlotte, North Carolina. In 1993 she earned her M.F.A. from Virginia Commonwealth University. She is the most recent in a long line of quilters from Laurens County, South Carolina. She lives and works in Richmond, Virginia, surrounded by the quilts of her grandmothers.

MICHAEL MCFEE has published four books of poems: *Plain Air* (1983), *Vanishing Acts* (1989), *Sad Girl Sitting on a Running Board* (1991), and *To See* (1991), the latter a collaboration with photographer Elizabeth

Matheson. His poems appear regularly in *Poetry*, where *Cold Quilt* was first published, and other leading magazines. He is a native of Asheville, North Carolina, and now teaches poetry writing at University of North Carolina–Chapel Hill.

JOAN MCMILLAN'S poetry has been widely published, with current work in Love's Shadow from Crossing Press and New Virginia Review. She is the descendant of many generations of women who made quilts from both necessity and joy.

SANDRA MCPHERSON is the author of six books of poetry, the most recent of which are *Streamers* (Ecco, 1988) and *The God of Indeterminacy* (University of Illinois, 1993). She has curated two shows of her African-American quilt collection. She is Professor of English at the University of California at Davis.

ELIZABETH SPIRES was born in Lancaster, Ohio, in 1952. She is the author of three collections of poetry: *Globe* (Wesleyan, 1985), *Swan's Island* (Holt, 1985) and *Annonciade* (Viking Penguin, 1993). She lives in Baltimore, Maryland, and teaches in the Writing Seminars at Johns Hopkins and at Goucher College.

ANN STRUTHERS teaches at Coe College where she is the Writer-in-Residence. She has published widely in journals including *Poetry*, *The Hudson Review*, *The American Scholar*, and *Iowa Woman*. Her collection *Stoneboat* appeared in 1989 from the Pterodactyl Press. *The Alcott Family Arrives and Other Poems* is from the Coe Review Press.

MAY SWENSON (1913–1989) worked as a newspaper reporter, secretary, ghost writer, editor, and poet-in-residence, but always and mainly as a poet, publishing 450 poems in her lifetime. All of these are love letters to the world, for she loved life and rejoiced in celebrating it.

SUSAN TERRIS lives in San Francisco. She has been writing and publishing fiction and poetry for twenty years. Her most recent books, published by Farrar, Straus & Giroux, are *Nell's Quilt* and *Author! Author!* She is currently completing a poetry collection entitled *Parallel Lives*.

DINA VON ZWECK is a writer, poet, and author of children's books. Books of poetry include *Sam Shepard's Dog* and *Halloween and Other Poems*. She is the co-author of *American Victorian* (Harper & Row) and the author of *Make Zoup*; *I Am Dreaming*; *Imagine That!*;

and other books for children (Dell Publishing). Her short stories have appeared in *Helicon Nine* and *New Letters,* and her poetry has been published in various literary journals. *Venus Unbound* (Simon & Schuster) is her most recent book. She is the recipient of a Massachusetts Council-on-the-Arts grant (for poetry). She has received a writer's grant at Altos de Chavon (Artist-in-Residence Program), Dominican Republic, to complete *Dominga & The Talking River,* a novel.

DOROTHY WALL has taught poetry and fiction writing at San Francisco State University and Napa Valley College. She currently teaches fiction writing at University of California–Berkeley, Extension. She is co-author of *Speaking of Voice: A Fiction Writer's Guide* (St. Martin's Press). Her poems, book reviews, and articles have appeared in numerous publications.

MARILYN NELSON WANIEK'S third book, *The Homeplace,* was a finalist for the 1990 National Book Award. Her forthcoming book is called *Magnificat.* She lives with her family in Connecticut and teaches at the University of Connecticut.

CAROL BOSTON WEATHERFORD, a poet, essayist, and business writer, resides in High Point, North Carolina. A native of Baltimore, she holds an M.F.A. from the University of North Carolina at Greensboro. Her work has appeared in numerous publications, including *The Washington Post, Christian Science Monitor, Callaloo,* and *Calyx.*

ROBERTA HILL WHITEMAN is a poet, fiction writer, and scholar, recently completing a doctorate in American Studies at the University of Minnesota. Her first collection of poetry, *Star Quilt,* won the Wisconsin Writers Award in 1985. "Summer Girl," a short story, is included in *Talking Leaves: Contemporary Native American Short Stories;* her work is also included in *Braided Lives: An Anthology of Multicultural American Writing.* She is working on a second collection of poetry and prose, and a biography of Dr. Lillie Rosa Minoka Hill. A Wisconsin Oneida, Roberta teaches at the University of Wisconsin. She lives with her husband, Arapahoe sculptor Ernest Whiteman, and their three children.

Marvin Bell, "Quilt, Dutch China Plate," *Southwest Review,* Volume 70, Spring 1985.

Joseph Bruchac, "Walking in November Across the Stream to the Sweat Lodge," *Long Memory.*

Obema, Onasbruck, Germany, 1989.

Martha Christina, "Crib Notes," *Zone 3,* Spring 1987.

Stephen Corey, "Quilts," *The Last Magician.* Huntington, New York: Water Mark Press, 1981;

reissued by Wesley Chapel, Florida: Swallow's Tale Press, 1987.

Anne George, "Quilting," *Wild Goose Chase.* Birmingham, Alabama: Druid Press, 1985.

Andrew Hudgins, "Patchwork," *The Glass Hammer.* Boston: Houghton Mifflin, 1994.

First published in *Shenandoah,* Fall 1992.

Larry Levis, "The Quilt," *Winter Stars.* Pittsburgh: University of Pittsburgh Press, 1985.

Michael McFee, "Cold Quilt," *Vanishing Acts.* Frankfort, Kentucky: Gnomon Press, 1989.

First published in *Poetry,* Volume 149, October 1986.

Joan McMillan, "Annabelle Cain McMillan, grandmother," *Bristlecone,* Spring/Summer 1990.

Sandra McPherson, "Quilt Top Discovered at the Muskogee Flea Market and Found to Contain

Blocks Resembling Certain Designs of Descendants of Maroons in Suriname,"

The God of Indeterminacy. Urbana/Champaign and Chicago, Illinois:

University of Illinois Press, 1993.

Elizabeth Spires, "Crazy Quilt," *Swan's Island.* New York: Holt, Rinehart and Winston, 1985.

First published in *The Yale Review,* Volume 72, October 1982.

May Swenson, "Under the Baby Blanket," *Motherwords.* New York: Knopf, 1987.

First published in *Antaeus* 44, Winter 1982. Copyright May Swenson

and used with permission of the literary estate of May Swenson.

Susan Terris, "Forgiveness," *The Sow's Ear Poetry Review,* Volume 5, Number 3, Fall 1994.

Dorothy Wall, "The Quilters," *Echoes,* Number 27, Winter 1992-93.

Marilyn Nelson Waniek, "The Century Quilt," *Mama's Promise.* Baton Rouge: Louisiana State

University Press, 1986.

Roberta Hill Whiteman, "Star Quilt," *Star Quilt.* Duluth, Minnesota: Holy Cow! Press, 1984.

Copyright by Roberta Hill Whiteman. Reprinted by permission of the author and publisher.

Old family quilts—particularly an unfinished Crazy Quilt top—inspired Felicia Mitchell's interest in quilting. A poet, critic of contemporary poetry, and scholar, Felicia is currently Associate Professor of English and Director of the Writing Center at Emory and Henry College, Emory, Virginia. Felicia's articles about contemporary poets have appeared in *Mid-America Review, Pheobe, The Southern Quarterly,* and *Dictionary of Literary Biography.* Her poetry has been published widely in such journals as *Spoon River Quarterly, Oxford Magazine,* and *Haight Ashbury Literary Journal,* as well as in anthologies, most recently *bite to eat place: an anthology of contemporary food poetry and poetic prose* (Redwood Coast Press). Her scholarly work has appeared in *College Composition and Communication, Issues in Writing, Women's Studies Quarterly,* and *Women and Language.*

Felicia lives in the mountains of Virginia with her husband and son.